4 poets

4 poets

Daniela Elza, Peter Morin,
Al Rempel, Onjana Yawnghwe

Poetry – Drafts – Translations – Interviews – Poetics

#1 New BC Poets Series

Mother Tongue Publishing Limited
Salt Spring Island, BC
2009

LIBRARY AND ARCHIVES CANADA CATALOGUING IN PUBLICATION

4 poets : Daniela Elza, Peter Morin, Al Rempel, Onjana Yawnghwe / illustrations by Joe Rosenblatt.

(New BC poets ; #1)
Includes 4 poems translated into French, Bulgarian, Tahltan and Thai.
ISBN 978-1-896949-03-1

1. Canadian poetry (English)--British Columbia. 2. Canadian poetry (English)-- 21st century. I. Elza, Daniela, 1967- II. Rosenblatt, Joe, 1933- III. Title: Four poets. IV. Series: New BC poets ; #1

PS8295.5.B7C64 2003   C811'.60809711   C2009-902672-4

Book Design by Mark Hand

Cover: *Landscape & Memory*, 2005, 68″ x 54″, acrylic on canvas by Ian Thomas.

Drawings on paper, pen and ink, 2009, by Joe Rosenblatt.

Printed on Rolland Enviro 100 Natural 100% recycled.

Mixed Sources
Cert no. SW-COC-001271
© 1996 FSC
FSC

BRITISH COLUMBIA
ARTS COUNCIL
We acknowledge the support of the Province of British Columbia
through the British Columbia Arts Council

Printed and bound in Canada by Friesens

Published by:
Mother Tongue Publishing Limited
290 Fulford-Ganges Road
Salt Spring Island B.C. V8K 2K6 Canada

phone: 250-537-4155   fax: 250-537-4725
www.mothertonguepublishing.com

Represented by the Literary Press Group in Canada

Introduction

The journey at the beginning and at the end of one's creative life is often the most difficult. These are times when you either need a supportive hand up and outward as an emerging poet, or as an older poet whose life's work is often forgotten, could use a hand back from the disappearing l/edge.

Our "New B.C. Poets" series intends to do just that. It will alternate between a combo of new, then older poets, showcasing their work in a fresh and stimulating format. Each volume will contain more than a dozen poems from each poet, drafts/ worksheets, translations of selected poems, statements on poetics, as well as author interviews and photographs.

The first title in this series, *4 poets*, brings the distinct and vibrant work of emerging poets Daniela Elza, Peter Morin, Al Rempel and Onjana Yawnghwe to a wider audience and invites your delving and listening, your response and remembering, your ear and your heart.

Mona Fertig
Publisher

Contents

The Poets

DANIELA ELZA

for my parents
за мама и татко

"The birch branch is an intuition
meandering endlessly toward a clear idea."
—Tim Lilburn

in the flicker of   (time
for Danijela Gašević

in this moment   where the sun
finds its way   through the mist

to the river.   lights up   this spot
for you.   where branches curl   stark

against sun beams

            ripples   flicker toward you

            outlining rocks—

their long green moss   bowing

at the edge   to drink.

even the sludge   brown water   looks

beautiful   in this fan of   sudden light

that found you
                    (h e r e.

your eyes dilate with   Now

        with what is   passing.

this river   is not time.

in the shutter of   your eye

            it is   a l w a   y s.

            *

the way trees   lean in

                 over   the flowing

as if trying to make it   into the frame

          of your memory.

                         they want to stay.

keep   calling to you.

and you will   (t h i n k   you are

          coming back
                         as you come forward.

          and you will   keep coming here

not because of   this moment

          (that will never be

                 *

again).

                 but because

          here

what is

                         remembered

          (is

          to be

                 understood

                         for the first time.

on the way to Sophia

it is not that there is   such a theory:
simple   unified   beautiful. we are

on an overnight train to   Sofia
and uncertainty hurts.   I cannot see much of

Serbia in the night   but my reflection.
in my mind   the images from yesterday

impose themselves
                    on the speeding darkness.

the houses—   all look the same
and the fields   and fields of corn—

a kind of   certainty
          the mind clings to.   develops
its negatives on
          the order   of things   past

the train's dirty window.   last night
they took a young man off   the train

in a language   I almost   understood.
(no visa.   no money.   non-negotiable.)

stepped him into

the black canvas   of his   n o w h e r e.
somewhere   someone waiting   for him to arrive.

*

today lulled by the rhythm   of metal on tracks
the swaying   from side to side   all I can do is

stare   into what rushes past:

a red volkswagen   crouched by a cornfield.
the houses I imagined passing   all night

(shuttered   caving in   roofs)
smokestacks in the distance   (and the trash.

along the railway lines shanty after shanty
hidden in groves.   a patchwork

of cardboard   cloth   carpet
aluminum   tin   tires.

ruined buildings that look like broken hearts:
their empty windows—   hollow sockets

staring back.

maybe that man (stamped   forbidden)
will sleep there tonight.   buttercups

sunflowers— fields   and fields of them.

and these houses—
abandoned.
their August trees   heavy with fruit.

all   the time   my mind   comforts

r a t i o   n   a   l   i   z   e   s:

but   someone is tending   the gardens
someone is   making   trash.

leaving—

*

our kind of certainty.

*"You see how we sleep under our tongues
like under a carpet—with our clothes on."*

—Georgi Gospodinov

breathing maps

under the linden tree   in full bloom
you say: these   trees are dreaming us.

their quantum thoughts

           leafing through the breeze.

in the shade   the scent is tantalizing
as we grope   toward

      how   Things   hang

together.

               *

most days   *you see*   *how we sleep*
under   *our tongues*

      in fear   of creating

chaos
      in some false sense   of order.

everyday   look into the mirror

        with vague recognition
and mild amusement

in a life that is not   an imitation

    but a triangulation

       toward   a point of

truth.
        we seek

          *

to find ourselves   on a canvas
in a 200-year-old house in the south of Bulgaria

(walls white-washed   with the forget-
                                        fullness

of its history)

we sleep   *like under a carpet—*
                              with our clothes on.

outside

the walnut tree   (from   my childhood)
                                        chopped down.

                    *

today   we add to this   canvas:
how   the clouds   lie

on the bosom of   Mt. Vitosha

this afternoon
                    after the rain.

                    *

still

                              most
                                        revealing

are those days   in which

                                        we fall

                    into each other

out of context   (trusting

the background   will fill itself in

if

                    we hold
                    tight enough.

interpreting the winds

for Margarita Vassileva

here   the three mountains   meet

here their winds come   to hold   council.

they settle down in the valley.   a small village

hosts their talks.

a good friend   lives here.

*

on   the   horizon   the   mist insists   on

erasure.

memory turns   silhouette

fades   and in places

disappears.

a matter of distance   this pilgrimage back—
part now

part remembered.

*

here the dead   are observed

with a ritual—   a slow procession

down winding   narrow lanes.

and the weddings   are loud

and full of dancing.   even cars will stop

for the vigorous *horo*　　　　　　weaving

　　　through the streets　　　to drums

　　　accordions　　　and pipes.

　　and if you happen　　upon a wedding

without being invited

　　　　　it is good luck.

they say:　god　　　invited you.　　　yes

　　this is the insistent Present　　　but also

　　　　　　　　Memory.

　　what the world is　　is how we age

　　　its grapes　in cellars

　　　　at a constant　12 degrees celsius.

　　　how we　drink them

　　　over tables　smooth with worry

　　at the end of the day　when　　*you have*

nothing　*in your grasp*　　*but perplexities*

and the best we can do ...　　*is*

share them　　*with each other.*

　　　　　*

the winds hold　　council　　here

　　where the three mountains　　meet.

　　　they may agree on the order　　　or disagree.

　　　they will　　eventually　move

　　　　mountains.

　　　today　　they are lovers　peacefully sleeping.

　　yesterday　they were legends:　feuding brothers

　　and sisters　who turned to rivers　forever

flowing away　from each other.

tomorrow   they will be   friends
    meeting   after many   years.

    *

    how to unpack   our histories?

    what to make   of them?

    (over tables of   heavy walnut

    over hand-made   bread

    a block of   white cheese   and

a bowl of   home-grown grapes)

    *

a matter of

    distance

    in time

    the taste

of the wine.

on the small back of breath

for Harold Rhenisch

hours of rhythm.   we climb.   left foot
right.   against   the crunch of

snow.   a tired song.   the moment
comes   when time   caves   in.

the body   wants   to give up.
to sing   a different   song.

to swallow   winter   whole.

                    *

I look for.   strength.   in the memory of
another day   when fog wrapped   around me

so thick   there could have been
nothing else.   a rope   stretched

between us.   only the tug   reminds
          I am not   alone.

then   wind   came:
          crystal pins in my face.

down   the rope line   echoes:

lost   lost   lost.

the building   drifting   in
and out.   seemed so close.   the sky

getting dark.

later that night   (feet up)   (a hot mug of
tea and rum)   we recount   over and over

what happened.   retold   the same old   jokes.

but   this time
                laughed   twice   as hard.

                        *

today   light

                                so much   light

the white   in the eye

                        hurts.

I put a foot
                in the step ahead

standing like   a boot.
                                        this taste of

winter
                in the lungs.

                        *

we arrive.   on the side of a snow bank
a doorway opens   and closes   against

the small   warm   breath   within.
we spread   food   on a long table.

the fire's little glow   binds us in the night

                singing.

I take some dishes to   the tiny kitchen
and see him.

the keeper   of this mountain hut

sitting   at the stove:

                        hair—   a winter waterfall
ancient)   eerily quiet)

                        a statue.   himself

lost   in the blizzard   of   a memory—

          (this feeling   (that he is   (absent.

                              *

after dinner   we step outside.

                    stare

at the dark dome. eyes wide.   tongues

stolen   by stars.

                              no meaning   *but*

what   *we find*   *here.*

                              s o   c l o s e.

if you stretched an arm   you can

pluck the light   right out of the sky.

I stay that way   for as long   as it takes

s t a r l i g h t

          to crystallize

                                        on the surface

                              of a thought
(one gets lost in).

walk in   through the narrow wooden door

          the glow of

(guitar (strings(mouths)   open)   in song)

          swallowing   us.

                              *

in the small hours of the morning   a crackling
wakes me.   dissipates   my nightmare:

we are searching for   the Seven Rila Lakes
no one remembers   seeing.

they say: they look like   footprints
up the mountain.   each named   after

something else.   under constant snow cover.
:doctored maps: :rumours of treasure:

:people who never returned: accompany us.

we dig snow graves.
                    lie in them
                                to keep warm.

the cold   so loud—
                            a rum bottle   breaking

next to my ear.

                        *

I lie there   (wide awake)

on the wooden boards.   listen

as the fire in the wood-stove   dies.   the wind
howls.   the men   snore.   we are

(

no purpose)   twelve people
in a small room   lined   all frozen

with sleep.

            (wandering through each others'   dreams.

I watch starlight   pace   the room   all night

passing light   from sleeping mouth

            to sleeping   mouth.

*"We have to understand the artistic process not only
as an attempted solution of a paradox, but as the paradox itself.
What one knows, one cannot say, and once said, it is no more the same."*

—Hans Hess

putting words	**in the mouth**	**of a picture**
the whole	picture is	just
part	of a bird:	how the
words		hunger for
the image.	where	
	black wings	touch
at the shoulders		the light
seeps	through	the seams
		of feathers
	and it looks	
like	a multitude	of paths
we are	each	
taking.		
but it is	right now.	right here
in this dark	nugget	of a crow's
		breast
this	moment	is a light-
beam	marking the	exiled
green	distance	with blue
possibility.		
I take		breath
from feather	to feather	
from shaft	to shaft.	hang onto
each.	while someone	is
running	their fingers	over
the barbs	interlocking	prosaic
	paths.	
		the arched
closing		
heavy		
doors		of our eyes.

inhabitions
for Dethe

put your head   on the bark of
this century   old tree.

surprise me.   stretch arms
around   as far   as they will   reach.

feel them   extend   into the crown
feet split   into fractal   roots.

now   push   a little further.   let
the tips of   your fingers   crawl

another inch.   last night   you
said   in your dream

I pulled a tree   out of   black
earth.   gave it to you.   all

you wanted   was something to eat.
still   you stepped inside   the trunk

and moved its limbs   as if   life
depended   on this dance.

on our accepting   the silence
of growing.   rings

as essential   as   the memories
that inhabit *us*.   our *home*.

inside   the skin of this   century
we stretch   our limbs.

uproot   one another   out of

deep   shadows.   become

resonant   drums.

in a tumble of feathers

DRAFTS, FINISHED POEM AND TRANSLATION INTO BULGARIAN

Sept. 17, 06   Is this Knowing?

I know something about you
and it is not in the photographs
and it is not in our conversations
which steers us in loud places

it is something I have found learned
~~about you from~~ in a my dreams
something I am not even willing
to admit I know in daylight

~~something~~ it is as sure as the snow
falling this morning
          I do not question it.
or this broken egg in my hands
     it is that ~~quiet~~
                    stubborn ~~and unnamed~~.
as the waterfall falling on the rocks
          It is that insistent
seeping through my fingers unnamed
          it is that quiet
to last minute ~~take shape~~
take flight   ~~wiggles it way out~~
the beat of a wing on my hand
The feeling remembered
as if in a dream.

Sept. 19, 06   Is this (knowing

I know sth. about you
and it isn't in the photographs
that we hold to remember
and it is not in our conversations
which steer us through loud ~~streets~~ in ~~market~~ squares
                      places

it is ~~what~~ something I ~~learn in~~ have picked up
in a dream   something I am not even
willing to admit.
          and it is as sure as the snow falling
this morning. it is that quiet
or the waterfall we sat under
       it is that insestent
or this broken egg in my hands
         I do not question it
it seeps through my fingers
       it is that elusive
yet in the moment when I think
                a bundle of feathers
it is gone   lost   it ~~moves~~ stirs
      in my hand
takes shape
the beat of a wing on my wrist
~~it is that certain.~~

Nov. 30th, 06

Is this (Knowing

I know something ~~about~~ you

and it isn't in the photographs
that we hold
          to remember

and it is not in our conversations
which steer us through the (noisy) streets

it is something I keep picking up
in dreams
         in images
and it is as sure of itself as a word is

or as the snow   outside falling
               this morning.
it is that quiet.
or the waterfall we may have sat under
        it is ~~that insistent~~
or or in the dream
~~or~~ this broken egg in my hands
I do not question it
  it seeps through my fingers
          and it is that elusive
yet the moment ~~&~~ I (think
         it is gone, lost
a bundle of feathers stirs in my palms
~~and the brush~~
~~again the beat~~ of a wing
         on my wrist
~~that could have been~~
      ~~in another dream..~~

in the dream?

hmmm...ite there
not quite there

in a tumble of feathers

I know   something   about you
and it isn't   in the photographs

we hold   to remember.

and it isn't   in our conversations
which steer us
        through noisy streets.

it is something   I keep   picking up
in r e v e r i e s   (in images

and it is as sure of itself
        as a word is.

or as the snow outside
       falling
         this morning.
     it is that quiet.

or the waterfall
     we may have sat under.
        it is that insistent.

or last night's dream—this broken egg
in my palms—
       (I do not question it.

it seeps through my fingers.   and

     it is that e l u s i v e.

yet   the moment   I think

it is gone   lost

a bundle stirs   into shape.   in my hands

full of feathers   (the knowing
in its parenthesis   of claws and beak.

видения   (под крилото на мисълта

translated by Daniela Elza

някак си   те   познавам.
не от снимките
            които пазим
                        за спомен.

не и от разговорите
            които ни упътват
                 из шумни улици.

то е нещо   което се п р о к р а   д в   а
в раз сея ни сияния
        в зар ея ни   образ и
            в за хлас нати х и м е   р   и

и то е толкова истинско
            колкото тези думи.

или като снегът
                който вали
                        тази сутрин.
толкова е тихо.

или като грохота   на водопада
                под който   някога сме седяли.

толкова е упорито.

или като това пропукано яйце
                        в ръцете ми—
в снощният сън—
        (в него не се съмнявам.
            и е толкова   неуловимо.

и в момента   в който   си по(мисля
че е загубено
                    у сещам трепет—
куп перца
между човчица   и нокти—

крилцата на това   по(знание
отново   погалват дланта.

Interview

1. What books, people, landscapes, fuel your poetry?

Nature, in its many fluid manifestations, is a considerable source of creative energy. Different geographies I have lived in and the wonder of their interconnectedness. Such a big idea. How to embrace it all and let it inhabit images and spaces in our daily life? How to approach this *all-at-once* that we cannot grasp? Sometimes it is musty books of philosophy. Gaston Bachelard with his *Poetics of Space* and *Poetics of Reverie* gave me permission to explore philosophical ideas poetically. So do Robert Bringhurst, Tim Lilburn and Jan Zwicky. So do my mentors, for which I am grateful. Listening to children speak, or friends. Our struggles. Each poem is a gesture, a partial grasping, an attempt at sneaking a peek at what is briefly eternal in things, their weblike rapture. And of course we fail, because words inevitably break down, simplify and make things appear separate. Still, we become better for trying.

2. How does a poem begin for you?

My poems have unruly births. Sometimes an image, an idea, a word or a line jumps out at me. It has to surprise me. It has to be charged. Some come at inconvenient times. Some I find like four-leaf clovers, suddenly, out of the corner of my eye. A gift. Others, I have to look for to find. Sometimes I have the idea, but it has not found its image, yet. And I have to wait. Once I had a line running through my head, but by the time I could write it down, it was gone. I got stubborn: Why should that stop me? I acknowledged its absence and still invited the poem, which begins: *The first line of the poem is/missing/in its wake/the sense of sudden water/the stillness of an egret...* then explores the idea. I am glad I persisted. The intention, the invitation, is key.

3. What is the importance of poetry in society? In schools?

Poetic attention is important to counterbalance our utilitarian and calculating ways. I feel that any honest and true exploration of the world begins with poetry. Then we break it down into disciplines. It is a way of inquiring, a way of knowing, an intimate conversation. Bringhurst says poetry knows more than the one who writes it. I agree. It may sound strange, but I learn from my poems. More intriguingly, he says that it may be the purest form of knowing. Bachelard says the poetic image bears witness to a soul which is discovering its world. Children have an open mind, a fresh way of seeing the world. That is what poetry asks of us. Why not sustain that, make space for it, allow for this discovery. How? By doing it ourselves. We do not all have to write poems, but I think we can all live poetically. It not only can be delightful, but transformative and empowering, an apprenticeship to freedom. School (and society) are already so steeped in rules that this kind of contemplative, playful, heart-ful attention is not only a breath of fresh air, but it can make us wiser. We need this in our world today.

4. Who are your favourite poets?

I have to say: Jorge Luis Borges, Rainer Maria Rilke, Lao Tzu, Octavio Paz, Nikola Vaptsarov, Anne Michaels, Wislawa Szymborska, Lyubomir Levchev, Robert Bringhurst, Aislinn Hunter, Jan Zwicky. Lately, Alison Pick and Sue Sinclair. The book called *Introduction to the Introduction to Wang Wei* by Pain Not Bread (written collaboratively by Roo Borson, Kim Maltman and Andy Patton) was quite an inspiration to me. I used to refer to it as my *poetry bible*.

Poetics

:the title escapes me:

try to own that   which changes   by the second.
there are many skies   in the corollaries of the heart.

we find rhyme sometimes   the best way   to woo them.
maybe   some book to tempt us   to look down   upon

the many *translations of sky*.

this poem needs   skies   to come   into the world
as much as the sky   needs   this poem   to worship it.

this poem needs the devotion   s   with which the sky is the same
and *always*   different.

you think   it's a minor affair   this coronary way. this birth
every moment.   this pre   -occupation with the slightest   of changes.

this *constant*   falling   in love.
is   love   *really*   blind?   I don't buy it.

this *kind* of love   is   seeing.   every   moment.
:a way: of circulating   the blood   through the four chambers

of the world.

        :this love:

is forgetting   yourself.   the very notion   of time.
if that is blind

             let *me*   be blind.

now try it.   try to own that   which changes
by the moment.

        try to own   that

which changes   *you*.

Daniela Bouneva Elza

Daniela Bouneva Elza was born in Bulgaria, and grew up in Nigeria. Moving between cultures and continents, she has always held a fascination for the diversity of words, and tinkers with them mostly to others' delight. After earning a Masters in English Philology from Sofia University, she lived in England for a year, then, for six years in Athens, Ohio, where she acquired her second Masters in Linguistics, and more importantly, her husband. In 1999, they immigrated to Canada and currently live in Vancouver with their two children.

Daniela has written for as long as she can remember in whatever language was available at the time. She likes big ideas, expressed concisely. It is no surprise then, that philosophy holds a special place in her pursuits, and poetry is her medium. She has a special interest in metaphor. For Daniela, poetry is a necessary part of the day, a place for serious play, a fierce meditation. She believes that writing a poem, and working on it, in turn alters the poet.

It is only in the last five years that Daniela has seriously started pursuing publishing her work; in that time it has won contests and has appeared in both literary and peer-reviewed publications. To date, she has released about a hundred poems into the world. She is currently compiling her first full-length manuscript.

ACKNOWLEDGEMENTS

Thanks for the epigraphs from the following texts: Tim Lilburn, *Living in the World as if it were Home*, Cormorant Books (1999), with permission. Salman Rushdie, *Haroun and the Sea of Stories*, Granata Books, 1991. Georgi Gospodinov/Георги Господинов, *Балади и разпади*, Bulgaria, Plovdiv: ЖАНЕТ 45 (2007). My translation. Hannah Arendt, *Life of the Mind*, Harcourt Brace Jovanovich (1978). Gregory Orr, *How Beautiful the Beloved*, The Virginia Quarterly Review (Spring 2007), with permission. Hans Hess, *How Pictures Mean*, New York: Pantheon Books (1974). Gaston Bachelard, *On Poetic Imagination and Reverie: Selections from Gaston Bachelard*, Dallas, TX: Spring Publications (1988).

The poem *inhabitions* was awarded 1st place by George Elliot Clarke in the Manitoba Writers'Guild *Friends* poetry contest (2007).

I would like to thank my parents Margarita and Peter Bounev, and my professor Alexander Shurbanov for help and advise with the translation of *in a tumble of feathers*, and Frank Lee (flee.com) for my photo. I would also like to thank Harold Rhenisch, Heesoon Bai, Carl Leggo, Nevena Giljanović, and my family, who in different capacities have accompanied, supported, and inspired me in the past few years.

PETER MORIN

These poems are dedicated to all my teachers, wherever you are.
Meduh for all your kindness.

A Map to the Exhibition.

1.

I want to learn my Tahltan language

I want to be able to speak in Tahltan to describe how I am feeling

I've started to know that the language lives and grows inside of me

I've started to know that the language grows up with me

2.

Rock Crow tells a rock story about the 1000 Crow darkness

In the story Rock Crow uses the words: *dechuwe[i], tudecho[ii], tak'kaje[iii], meduh[iv], soga sinla[v], sowah asinlah[vi] [vii]*

Crow/Man hears the cries of the animals and people, who are living in a world without light.

The Crow/Man investigates this world and finds a Father/Grandfather who is holding the light: the daylight, the sun, the moon, and the stars.

Crow/Man discovers the Father/Grandfather's home but it has no visible door in the darkness.

So, Crow/Man watches.

Crow/Man is good at watching.

Crow/Man turns himself into a pine tree needle, and places himself in the drinking water of the Father/Grandfather's daughter.

She drinks the water and swallows the Crow/Man. The young girl becomes pregnant with the Crow/Man. And eventually, the girl gives birth to a Crow/Man/Grandchild, who plays with the light.

When Crow/Man/Grandchild is strong enough, he steals the light away and releases it to the world.

The story tells you how to grow your own map. It tells you to look for these places and to put them into your heart space. And the story tells us to stop worrying about when we can return to our land *Worry ain't woh-thh'r it.[viii]*

Just know that wherever you are:

You are on your land

You are the names given by the land

Your footsteps are part of our spoken language

3.

Blanket of feathers
River of feathers
Rocks turn into Crows

There is a place in the territory where our two rivers meet
and the Crow has his house

This place has been important for our people because
we have gathered our food here for many thousands of years.

My great-grandmother's smoke house still stands here

This is a place of great moving
And a place of great living

When I stand near the water
watching *the river throw sand upon its banks*[ix]

I can't stop imagining that darkness
Before the Crow found that light

If I was in that darkness
How would I feel?

But it seems that the darkness wasn't darkness
until that Crow found that light

So I imagined that we were not afraid of the dark
Because there was no dark

And I imagined that that darkness was like walking through a thousand dark
feathers

And I imagined that we are constantly moving through
feather dark and feather light

4.

Things that I leave behind for Ravens:
Red Rocks
Red Cloth
Red Cloth Blindfolds
Red Earth Jacket
The language
Protection
And moccasins for the journey

If I return to look for the language
I have to look very closely at everything

Because I have collected many things and years
That can block up my eyes and ears

I have to look closely and pick up rocks, cloths, blindness,
and the earth jacket
like it is the first time

This will help me to acknowledge
That I have the language inside of me
That it is my language and I am able to speak it fluently

5.

four directions of language

The first lesson is that you have to work for your stories

The second lesson is that you have to walk out on to your land to do this work

The third lesson is that you have to protect what was given to you because eventually you will have to give it away

The fourth lesson is you are able to speak your language
Because it is your language

6.

Drum of rocks
Pictures of dancing Crows

Our books
Our reading
Our spoken language
Our living

[i]   I've included these words in the story Rock Crow tells, because they are an important aspect of my personal Tahltan lexicon. This is the word that communicates porcupine. This word is a very special word to me because it is the first word I feel that I learned in the language. I remember being at a store, and seeing porcupine quills, and I felt that I needed to buy them. Once I had them home, I wondered what I needed to do to make a porcupine quill choker for my sister. It was my mom that said this word. Then, I asked our grandmother what are the words for porcupine quill in the language. This represents my first real attempt at learning the language.

[ii] During my time as the language and cultural teacher at Denetia School, in Lower Post, I had the most amazing language experience from sharing what I knew with the students at the school. One thing I noticed was that we all felt stronger and more confident when we were speaking the language. So, I spent time designing fun ways to keep the learning interesting engaging for the students and myself. So, I made a language bingo game that the kids and I played one Friday afternoon. Unfortunately, I had made more call words then I had spaces on the cards, so the word tudecho was said a lot. It became one of my favorite words, even if the students hated hearing it.

[iii] Recently, I had the opportunity to bring my partner home with me to Telegraph Creek. It was one of my proudest moments to be able to share this special place with her. One of the important places on the reserve to go to was to visit my grandmother Violet. She is 82 years old and is of the last fluent speakers of the language. So. While I was there I was doing my best to share with her what I had been learning by being a language teacher. I told her I know two ways to say frog: tahk'effe, tah'kweje. So, she shared with me a third way: Tahk' kaje. And we spent the next twenty minutes working on my pronunciation. She said it's your language, you'll learn it easy if you want.

[iv] This has always been a word in the language that has been apart of my life. I couldn't tell you when I first learned it. You say this word to express your appreciation to someone who has done you well.

[v]   This is a word from the Kaska Dena territory. I learned it when I was there learning from the Kaska Dena. This is a lesson that they shared with me. You say this word to express your appreciation to someone has done you well.

[vi] There is an amazing speaker from Kaska Dena territory named Denis Porter. He is a fluent speaker of the language and is able to tell people like me–people on a learning path–things we need to know about the usage of these words. He tells us in a way that our mostly English tongues can understand and transform into original tongues. He told me this, you say these words when you are expressing your appreciation to someone who has done you well.

[vii] Since the words listed are from a spoken language, I've chosen not to rely on the linguistic spellings but more on how I would say them.

[viii] This is my grandma's voice.

[ix] This place is a place of description and language. It is honoured for how it has shaped our culture, community, and identity.

Land Stories.

1.

How do we tell the land's stories?

2.

I didn't know about Lower Post until I moved north. We were living in Watson Lake, which is about twenty kilometres away. It was winter, and I hadn't actually left the house for months. Eventually, Ga Ching comes home and says, "I met the principal at Lower Post and they are looking for a language and culture instructor." So, I applied and got the job.

I was there for a brief time. During my time there I met some teachers whose wisdom and stories have helped shaped my vision and my words.

3.

One elder named Mida told me some of the history of Lower Post. She told me that the community at Lower Post started in 1847 after a Trading Post put down roots near that slow bend in the river. After the HBC closed the other seven posts in the north the people decided to stay at Lower Post. So, since then, there have always been people near that slow bend in the river.
She also told me the Kaska at Lower Post were called Daylu Dena. She said they got the name Daylu because the white people couldn't understand when they said dollar. It wasn't because the Kaska weren't speaking clearly; it was because the white people weren't listening.

Dollar Dena, Daylu Dena.
Dennis told me that the Kaska at Lower Post are called *Little Mountain Kaska*. The elder said that *Little Mountain Kaska* is one of the seven dialects that make up the language group that is called Kaska Dena.
The kids at Lower Post call themselves *LPs forever*.

4.

Lower Post became a home for one of the residential schools. Like the trading post before it, the Residential School put its own roots beside that slow bend in the river. Today, most of the school has been pulled down. But we still know its there, even though we can't see it.

Eva told me about working in that school as a cook. She saw the nun hit her daughter. So she went after the nun.

Ripped her hat clean off, she said.

She never bothered my kid again.

Louise told me another story about some of the kids who went to that school. They would sometimes go to Whitehorse on trips. And she would sometimes supervise them at the friendship centre as an after school youth supervisor.

A whole class of them, she said.

I think most of those kids are dead now.

5.
At LP I see kids fly.

And everybody knows it.

And everyone honours them for it.

In the summer and in winter they fly.

Before school and after school they fly.

With shovels and brooms they fly.

With death upon death they fly.

Nothing seems to stop them.

6.

In LP a group of kids told me stories about skate boarding. They taught me about sk8ing so that I could hang with them.

I'd also been told stories about their skate boarding from their grandma Bernice. She said that in the summer they keep their skate park clean with stolen brooms.

And she said that in the long winter they would steal snow shovels and shovel out the snow, so that they could still continue their practice

On the sunny days, I'd see Bernice drive them to the larger skate park uptown in Watson and yell down to them the tricks she wanted them to perform.

She would be there with them until they were ready to go home.

7.

My personal favourite is when they do that rolling jump. That jump when they have to throw their arms up behind them for balance as they fall back to land. I think they look like eagles when they do this jump. When I think about those eagles I can't get sad, tired, or feel alone.

Those eagles have helped me to

see the horizon, how it breaks,

how it shatters when you fall back to the ground,

so hard that you have to throw your arms up

not for balance

but to get ready for the next jump.

The struggle isn't the body in the water.
The struggle is the body.

1.

I had two dreams about the crows outside my window.

In the first dream the larger crow yelled at me in crow language about how I should know better and that it was time to speak the language. The larger crow told me that she would help. She was my grandmother. I believed her. I yelled back in crow language.

In the second dream I reached down the crow's throat. The crow's body opened up like a flower. I was able to turn it inside out. Inside the crow's body was a most beautiful painting of the atom bomb cloud. The crow said look inside of my body for the answers to your struggles. Inside the body I saw the destruction.

2.

Teaching the language makes me nervous

Talk to them about the importance of our language

Don't let on until later that I am also learning

Keep their attention

Make promises of fun

Make promises of fun

Put on the tape

Step one: put on the tape
so that they can hear the language
in the classroom

Step two: put on the tape
so that you can hear the language
in the classroom

3.

Ahda Bes
(Eagle Knife)

Cha Ch'a'an
(Rain Arrowhead)

Dih Dleze
(Grouse Grizzly)

Dzudze Etsen
(Bird Meat)

Tehk'efe Gah
(Frog Rabbit)

Ghanje Hih
(Canada Goose Mountain)

Ihti Jani
(Bow Here)

Kuk'a K'os
(Cup Cloud)

Labat Luge
(Mitts Fish)

Men Nogha
(Lake Wolverine)

Ogisogi Espane
(Outside My Friend)

Sas Shal
(Black Bear Fish Trap)

Tudecho' Dzudzet'oh
(Mallard Duck Bird's Nest)

Tli Tl'oge
(Dog Grass)

Tsa Ts'ede
(Beaver Blanket)

Dlune Gwel
(Mouse Packsack)

Yuka ezes
(Northern Lights Hide)

4.

The kids and I started to spend a lot of time telling stories. We would talk about what we did on the weekend, or we would tell stories about what we did on the days when I wasn't at school.

Some kids would tell stories about where they went, or what they watched on TV, or what games they played on their computer.

Some kids would tell stories about being happy, or being sad, or getting into fights with their best friends, brothers and enemies.

One day, we talked about hunting.

The first kid tells the story about this one time he was hunting with his cousin and he uses the Indian words during his story to communicate to me what animals he was hunting.

The second kid tells me another story about hunting, and he uses the Indian words during his story to communicate to me what animals he was hunting.

The next kid tells me a story about his cousin going hunting and he uses the Indian words to communicate to me what animals his cousin was hunting.

The next kid tells me about fishing and he uses the Indian words to communicate to me that he was fishing in our territory.

One of the two young girls in the class tells me a story about owning horse and riding horse and she asks me how do we say horse in our language before she finishes the story.

One kid tells a story about hunting with his cousin and uses the white people words to describe the animals that he was hunting, but before he finishes his classmates tell him to use the Indian words.

And this is our good medicine.

This is what is meant by working to keeping strong.

These words are *Tses'kiye*.
These words are *Chi'yone*.

This is written on my body.

Right now I am lost.

In the dream is my grandmother,
my grandfather who died before I was born
and several others.
They tell me I am Tahltan
And I nod my head

I will take a rock like she said,
I will find the right rock and place it on my hurt.
I will walk holding the rock on my place of hurt.
I will ask the grandmother rock for help.

Help me to release this pain
I will say
Help me to release this pain so that I may start again
I will say
Something has been stolen from me
I will say
I will work hard to start again, grandmother please help me.
I will say

I will walk with this rock on my place of pain
Until I find a river, there I will put the grandmother rock,
To be washed
To be washed of my grief
And to be safe from the weight.

I will say joy harjo prayers to the creator, to the grandmother,
to the grandmothers and grandfathers, to the river, to the earth.

I am looking for answers,
I can no longer bear this weight

And I will make a blanket
And I will wear it in the places where it belongs.
And I will share this story with you if you ask

And in a good way, the grandmother will smile.

I keep inviting my Grandmother to my art shows.

I remember holding her hand
Thinking that I was holding her weight

It wasn't until I was older
That I realized she was holding on so tight.

She was saving me.

Our Land Languages

Drafts and Finished Poem in English and Tahltan

In the Tahltan Children's dictionary, *Den ke'eh Didene* is translated to mean teacher.

Den ke'eh didene
den ke'eh

den

ke'eh

den (pronounced den)

implies a body or a speaker

ke'eh (prounounced with a small sounding k stop then eh)

in connection with den implies a speaking voice

Dene (pronounced Den Neh) is the word used to indicate person

*ke (*pronounced keh) is the word that indicated foot or feet

ke'eh shown together implies travel over distance

di dene this is the word to identify the People

di (pronounced dee) indicates 'this' as in reference to person

dih (pronounced Dee) implies knowing as in *I know this or I know that*

dene (prounounced den neh)

dene is the word that indicates person

Den'ke Didene: a person who is a speaker of the language is a teacher.

4/10

Our ~~Land~~ Languages

~~In the Tahltan Children's dictionary, Den ke'eh Didene is~~
~~translated to mean teacher.~~

What does it mean to translate the land?

These words ~~achieve~~ a different meaning ~~when~~

~~put into English~~

~~when~~ I hear these words ~~from my heart place~~

~~I know that~~ they are my foot steps

~~back~~   forth.

den ke'eh

den   forward

ke'eh   Speak

den

a body or a speaker   forward.

ke'eh

a speaking voice

Dene

person

ke

foot

ke'eh

What does it mean to translate the land?
I hear these words
they are my footsteps

our travel over distance

di dene

the People]ᐟ

di

that know

The people who know
how to travel over great distance
are speakers of the language

Den k'eh Didene

Den k'eh Didene
that know
the people
who travel
over great
distance.

my grantfather
used to walk
from Clay gaw heen
to tat'lah

this is what happened
before the Road

Dennis Porter would
walk from Lower Post
to Watson Lake
every day
he is a speaker of
the language.

Our Land Languages.

In the Tahltan Children's dictionary, Den ke'eh Didene is translated to mean teacher.

These words achieve a different meaning when

put into English

when I hear these words from my heart place

I know that they are my foot steps

back

den ke'eh

den

ke'eh

den

a body or a speaker

ke'eh

a speaking voice

Dene

person

ke

foot

ke'eh

our travel over distance

di dene

the People

di

that know

The people who know
how to travel over great distance
are speakers of the language.

Den k'eh Didene.

Interview

1. When did you begin to write poetry and what inspired you to continue?

At some point in my writing there was a strong shift to writing poetry. For years I was writing down thoughts, sentences, reflections that did not necessarily connect into a coherent form but were written specifically as a way to organize my thoughts. I was also writing a lot of ideas/sentences that I was breaking into parts, then collecting them into long list poems because I felt I needed to disguise my thoughts into an abstract form only I could read.

Then I found Joy Harjo.

I found in reading her work a strong connection to the inherent power of words and a connection to how these words can create a shift in the energy of the universe. Joy Harjo wrote with seriousness and service to her chosen words. She wrote prayers for those of us who were still looking for the words to make our own. Her example inspired me to work harder to build connection between myself and the words, and between the words and the universe.

2. What are the most important things you keep in mind when distilling a poem?

I chose poetry as one of the forms to aid in my explorations of meaning in my Tahltan Nation culture and community practices. The way of words, their connection to each other, and their connection to the idea are focused on my experience of building a stronger relationship to meaning–through all of the darkness (colonialism, oppression, genocide, racism) that can cloud the beauty of building community and cultural practices when living in the city. When writing these poems, I focus on being true to my Tahltan community practices, and being true to my community members who have showed me these wonderful practices.

3. Do you think poetry will ever fully enter the mainstream, e.g., be read in the legislature, before concerts, sports, on the news, at public ceremonies, on ferries, in pubs…?

For me, I understand poetry as mainstream. In our urban and rural indigenous communities, the emphasis on having strong words has always been an important cultural value. There has always been an emphasis on being true to your words, and understanding that they have cause–because once they are spoken you can't call them back. This has always been a way of being for my family and my community, the connection to poetry for me is about connection of words to intention.

4. Who are your favourite poets?

Joy Harjo, Simon Ortiz, Chrystos, Sherman Alexie, Dionne Brand, Roberta Hill, Whitman, Chitra Banerjee Divakaruni, June Jordan, Mitsuye Yamada, Ikkyu, Robert Davis, Shirley Bear, Faye Heavyshield, Gregory Schofield, Marlene Nourbese Philip, Hone Tuwhare, Souvankham Thammavongsa, Peter Blue Cloud, Anne Carson, Adrienne Rich, Nela Rio, Joseph Dandurand, Haunani-Kay Trask, Dunya Mikhail, LeRoi Jones, Ray A. Youngbear, Pablo Neruda, Leslie Marmon Silko, Thich Nhat Hanh, Fred Wah, Joanne Arnott, Grandma Dinah, Grandma Violett, Grandma Emma, Grandpa John, Grandpa Walter, Uncle Eddie, Aunty Helen, Aunty Doreen, Aunty Anne, Aunty Irene, Uncle Clifford, Aunty Nellie, Aunty Louise, Aunty Dinah, Aunty Anna, Willie Brown, Uncle Sidney, Aunty Gracie, Uncle Scott, Uncle Robbie, Uncle Leonard, Uncle Chris, Uncle Vernon, Uncle Jerry, Uncle John, Uncle Paul, Uncle Bruce, Uncle Tom, my Mom and Dad. This list could go on… but without these people I would not have been able to find a way to write.

Poetics

There are so many poetics in the First Nations' community. We have storytelling, singing, dancing, speech making, drum making, hide tanning. These are all places in the practice of our traditional knowledge that require a loving relationship to meaning, and require practice to become proficient at the building of forms. I have endeavoured to develop a better relationship with language, both spoken and written, as an extension of those traditional knowledge practices.

Our words have power. I have heard them described as a process, as a harpoon thrown out into the water to gather substance, then pulled back into our possession. I have heard the process described as a thunderbolt of energy that fills the heart and connects heart to heart to heart. And I have heard that we have a responsibility to witness words.

A struggle to contend with while growing up was how distant English words felt. This was evident throughout most of my grade school/high school/university education. I was not close to these English words. I had a distrust of them. These words had not done much to support our aboriginal experience. And yet, I also felt very dependant on them because they were there. My writing to this point has developed as a result of exploring themes of de-colonization through my desire to return to Tahltan language, of wanting to build a stronger relationship to speaking our language with confidence.

Our language is important in how we relate our experiences to one another, as well as establish meaning. Our words have not been lost. Our words are waiting for us. I am choosing to pick up these words and use them to speak. These words are what our grandmothers used to speak to us with strong purpose. Now that I've been looking for our words, I've been finding Tahltan words everywhere on the ground–near the river, left lying around during fishing time, in the store aisles, on the road and at the mall. The writing is now a record of the process I make each day towards a deeper connection with our Tahltan language and culture. My voice is Tahltan. It comes from the land, from the traditional Tahltan territory. I work towards learning our stories, songs and language.

Peter Morin

Peter Morin is from the Crow Clan of the Tahltan Nation. For the past ten years in his creative work, Peter has been developing a creative practice that directly reflects the Tahltan worldview taught by his elders. His work with Indigenous language started when he was hired to be the Language and Culture teacher for Denetia School in Lower Post. The goal of his work during this time was to create a space that acknowledged cultural sharing, where students would be able to share their cultural knowledge and to have acknowledgement of their community knowledge. It was during this time that Peter began to see the power of our communities' stories in practice. The stories were coming in everyday, and they needed to be acknowledged and honoured. The writing comes from the ability to see these stories and to combine the creative approach as a way to support positive change for our community.

ACKNOWLEDGEMENTS

I want to say sogha sin'lah to the people of Lower Post BC. The time I spent there in the community was very important to me.

I want to also say, that I chose to use the names of some of the storytellers from Lower Post in my poem as a way of showing respect 'dene a nezen' to those storytellers/didene k'eh from Lower Post, who were kind to share some of their truths with me during my short time visiting.

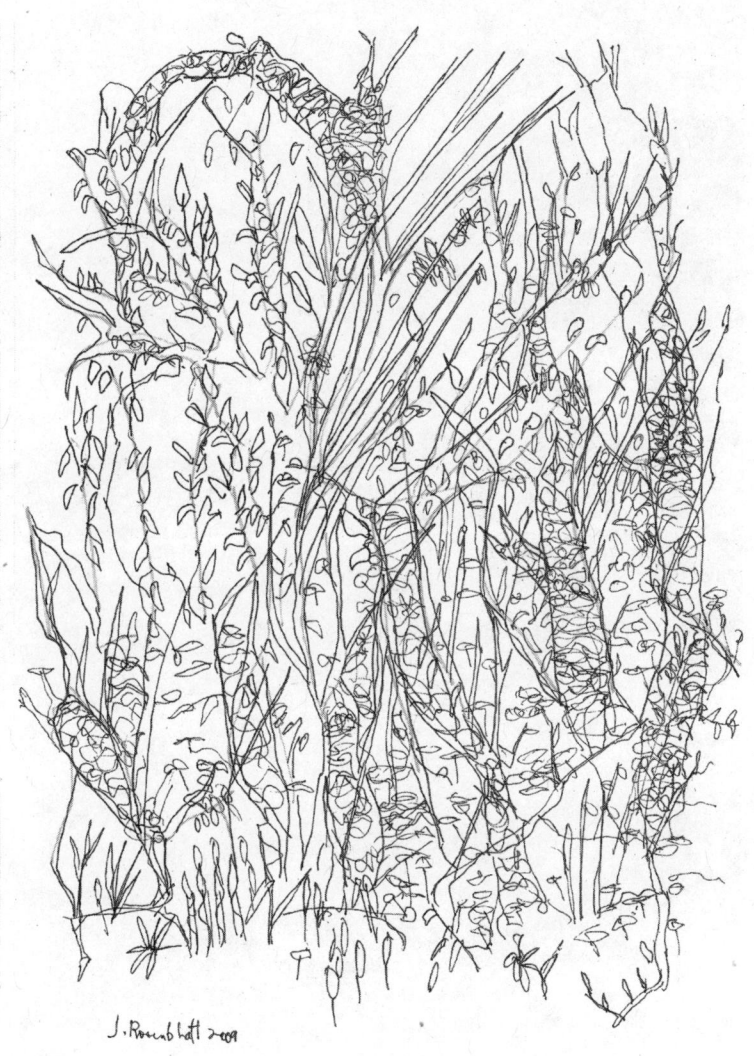

J. Rosenblatt 2009

photo: Jayson Hencheroff, Focal Point Studios

AL REMPEL

For Linda and Eloise, my two loves

A Few Lines for Prince George

thirteen years old and I'm exhuming the contents of the World Book Encyclopedia
right down to the transparencies in Volume 9, the Human Body vascular and muscular—

imagine a great lake overhead, dammed up by volcanic rock and the remains
of the last ice-age, maybe 10,000 years ago, until one day the whole thing busted loose—

stripping off skin, tendons, veins until I reached the female reproductive system
a big let-down, only the barest suggestion of breast, no more revealing than bulges—

carved through the hills, left Carney and Connaught standing tits-up
sliced off cut-banks of sand, exposed the bedrock on Foothills near First Avenue—

under sweaters and blouses and striped t-shirts, confusing the hell out of me
but there was no way I'd ask mom; barely survived the lesson on circumcision—

every day we cut along the smooth curve and arc of ancient river-benches
the maps in our head already determined, wheels thrumming over floodplains of gravel—

so I'm burying my head in books, read about a convict who gave his body over to science
after navigating the long corridors and corners between death-row and the chamber—

imagine walking the same footpath as your ancestors did to your hunting grounds
maybe along the trail to Shelley on the east side, crossing over the Fraser only in winter—

frozen as hard as bone for two days, 'the body' was cut into 1878 slices
each the thickness of a fingernail, and resurrected in virtual images nine months later—

or in late summer, when the sockeye salmon were running, setting up camp
spearing fish after fish after fish, all of us greedy for life, until the river bled—

flipping the pages from Human Body to Heart: one pump to move blood to the lungs
the oxygen sapped by the cells, the other to collect waste products from every cell —

imagine the exhaust of a two-stroke chainsaw, truckloads of logs piled layer after layer
a swarm of beehive burner smoke mixing with fog and mist off the Fraser River—

tried to clear off the emotional detritus of the dead and the dying: stick to the facts of life
replace the light at the end of the tunnel with a flash of neurons sparking every pathway—

the ladies at night on the corner of George St. and Second Ave, bosoms pushing out
looking for enough coin, the darkness closing in as they slump against the brick wall—

the embalmer injects the corpse with formaldehyde, methanol, and ethanol
the body is then dressed in his best blue suit and laid out for a postmortem viewing —

men piled up ten deep along the 50 foot bar of the Hotel Northern pass their dollar forward
wait for the slosh of whiskey glasses to work their way back with no chance of change—

the embalming process usually involves 4 parts: arterial, cavity, hypodermic and surface
closing the mouth and eyes, and any necessary shaving, is known as setting the features —

or in rings around tables like bark, sawdust hanging from beards and moustaches
the smell of oil and gas and pitch wafting into the middle of booze-fueled arguments —

hold a mirror just above the victim's mouth, look for condensation
take a pulse by placing two fingers firmly on the wrist, check for signs of life.

Landscape

folded hands, interlocked knuckles, cupped —
can only old people sit this still?
let their eyes drift the way a gull
surfs the length of shore?

in the distance a long line made of muted blue and gray refuses to resolve…

there is no mention that place shifts
as often as a grain of sand

does the land hold the ocean?

the fingertips long for a photograph
tucked four-square in
against the threaded, black page —

not for a snapshot in time, though that was once
wanted, but for a surface
to touch

the pinking-shear edges, the roll and wash of wave

we suppose looking is important
the seeing surely
but for the way the light plays out long after the cane
is picked up and shuffled on
                            the way
the gull returns with the tide

Oscar Lake

                smooth rounds
white basalt on sphagnum
club-moss and toad-pelt
questionable mushrooms

a clear view of the lake...

                I've got ripples
on the surface of my cortex
an intersect of bliss and rosehips
on prickly stems

did we deserve this?

                a deft hand
takes us out with the crows
who keep track of the layers
winter makes

we presume.

let us close our eyes
just this once
                and lean back

Yellow Pear

she left
a yellow pear
on the window-sill
you thought she was
saving it for later
to get even riper
and glanced
at it often
as   you
made love,
turns out
she wasn't

A Day on Bednesti Lake

these silvered moments
the sun
     a bell-jar sky
breathing moisture
          leaf-metal

how could this bird?

the day
without wings
not really
     but gossamer

aslant in the glass
the glint
     wine-throated
and thrumming

ideas
the ascent
a seed-headed drift
threaded

the web across
        lake-side
        lake-wet
        lake-

eggs recently hatched
the expanse
     terrestrial
a project

let out of the bottle
the glass
     as green as
and fishing

clams for stones
the berries
        under in the scrabble
over

it floats
the fire of it
      letters
smoke-charcoal

the embers
      deciding
when to go

Fretting Winter

The semis whistled through the sulphur of frozen air. The sounds of high-tension wires snapping. We walked with short, quick steps. What else could we do?

The crows pecked and pulled a song of thread that ran clear through to spring. Or so we hoped. We wrapped cable TV around ourselves to keep warm.

The birches were birches and nothing more. We bickered with the thinness of the fourth dimension.

Columns of smoke tunneled through holes in the sky. We tried to cap and lid our pillboxes of fear. The smell of it curled up with the dogs outside. We came unstrung.

The car filled up with carbohydrates. We got good at circular reasoning. Shoveled out the ifs with the snow. Then stuffed our faces.

The shadows of buildings slanted across the city. We hop-scotched over cracks clutching amulets.

There was evening and there was morning, the first of too many days. We knew that the wind-chill numbers were all made up. Like the price of gas. Like the words we exchanged in bed.

The last thing we wanted to come down was the wires. We would have done anything. We worshipped the hydro men in their crow's nest machines. Waited in the darkness.

Shiver In

we could shiver into the skin of winter
tap-tap the last clutch of leaves
from within

in spite of the hushing hissing forest

listen: birch   birch   aspen   aspen
       birch   birch   aspen   aspen

the anatomy of the hills are laid bare:
a rock doubles as sternum
heaves slightly

we could breathe ourselves upright
bone clicking on bone
woody-green lungs
                   filling up

listen: birch   birch   aspen   aspen
       birch   birch   aspen   aspen

the world is varicose
at least as far as the knees
                   a pulse

we can feel under the veneer

last night I dreamt I was a birch
felt the sap set deep
into the marrow of my shinbones

woke up with yellow and gold
leafing open in my palms

Go Down to the River

go down to the river and swallow it whole, roll the rocks around
in your mouth, pocket some in your cheeks, let the silt and grit get caught
in your teeth and grind it in, taste the blessed mountain of it, eat the bark
scaled at the mill upstream, suck back the slurry of the paper-plant waste,
chew on the trash of campfires gone bad, cans of cheap beer
and shards of glass, choke back the roach burns, the good-time condoms,
make this river yours, gulp it down, the last of the Coho eggs, the chin-hair
of the moose knee-deep in algae, tamarack needles drifting off
the silken dive of the loon, the yellow pollen pushing at the shore,
the dead cedar fronds like lace on your tongue, make this water holy water,
stick your dirty thighs in it, drink deep from last year's winter,
the crackling of the lakes, the snap of branches, the ice chattering
over beaver dams, the gun-shy grouse, chuck it down the hatch,
don't spit it out, the mushroom spore, the frog sperm — get it down, get it down

Fidelity

take the time you bent to fiddle with the radio dial in dad's old Buick —
seeking a clarity you thought you could have, should have,
that the Stones had, in their tight-fisted picks: it's a gas, gas, gas,
and the steering-wheel with its odd way of travelling, a loose tie-rod
dad said later, your eye on the red line instead of the yellow,
was it ninety-one point four or point five? the tread biting hard
on the gravel, the wheel once casual under your wrist suddenly
a sharp twist, a giant snake, an off-weight hammer, took hold
of you, tore into the red-osier dogwood, the foxtail,
the sapling alder slapping at the chrome bumper, the fender,
that damn tie-rod, no better now than a dislocated shoulder,
and you, the electric shock of it racing between heart and eye,
the arm locked at the elbow, as if by sheer physical force
you could steer the course of the universe, guitar strings zinging,
the double-thump of the bass-drum deep inside your chest-box,
the imagined mess of metal and dash-board plastic and birch-bark,
and the flip-over tumble between a blur and black-out,
the wheel on the driver's side spun free of bone-on-bone
and the hard-hollowed socket of reason, yet somehow you pulled
it back, mom said it was angels, but she always says that,
dad said why the devil didn't you keep your eyes on the road, mom said
leave it alone or he'll cry and you–you were still shaking on the davenport
craving a smoke and not wanting to think about it, or go there, instead
wanting to push it off, to take the keys off the hook, to take another spin
around the block first chance you got — to drive like nothing ever happened.

Vehicle

tried to duck behind the t in truck
behind the windscreen of c in car, the b
in brow pulled tight across the skull
tried to hide behind the d and hard g
in dark sunglasses, behind q in squint
but most of all behind the hard c, the stab
of k in fuck you too, words like capsules
pushing down the road, pushing down
the lump in your throat, hard-shelled
and crustacean, the soft bits of language stuck inside
wanting to be cracked open, sucked dry
the tongue praying uh-uh for the aphrodisiac
of I love you, the shape of each word
spilling out of the vehicle onto the wet grass
in a slippery mess of arms, hair, and legs
the keys still dangling in the ignition
the door-ajar warning bell faintly ringing

Saskatchewan Glacier

they say there's an old army jeep
trapped under the ice somewhere
after it made a sudden wrong turn;
the glacier inches its retreat and one day
water will leak from the cracked dash
and drip free from the gas gauge

we follow the tracks the jeep once made
until the river cuts it down into one lane
and then nothing, forcing us into the willow;
we snake in and out of burned-out fire-pits
and edge alongside old river-benches
until we round the corner and glimpse
the shimmer of ice dissolving

the valley floor is a scramble
of rocks and stones and boulders;
we lose sense of scale and the push of time;
with the wind at our ears
we're unable to hear the waterfall ahead
unable to hear ourselves except at close range

we walk farther, pulled in by the glacier
which slips in and out of view behind a ridge;
surely we could reach out and touch the ice
but the lake at the toe stops us

we play on its narrow shore, pick rocks
wash them off in the blue-grey water

this is the source, the ancient of days
and everything, even the water, looks old;
we trace our fingers in the silty clay

One Year Folds Into Another

he slaps his big fat thumb down in the middle of the rings
and pushes out a clear path through the sawdust to the edge:
feel it
      he orders

in ten minutes we will get up from this sanctuary
of archives and he will nod to a saw
and we will fall all day until my knees
buckle and my hands burn

a chipped fingernail
picks at the bark:
this is the cambium
in here
      these last ten years
all tight with growing old

when the sun tops the trees stuck on the ridge
I'll need to run to keep up
we'll push out of the woods onto an empty stretch of gravel road
and he will sit down on a log
cross one leg over his knee
balance a thermos cup on the other
and begin to whittle a toothpick

we hammered that slope
laid her flat all afternoon mostly
pine and spruce and the odd fir
screaming over the hinges

took a beating in '68
      he shouts above the roar
and I can't tell whether he means him
or the war
or the scar in the stump his thumb passed over
on its way to the outer edge

Part-Time Prospector

DRAFTS, FINISHED POEM AND TRANSLATION INTO FRENCH

bob's a gold-panner on the side
knows secret spots on the Fraser
        hidden entries
arteries of gold sifted through gravel
knows spade:
the swirl-sounds on tin
the filtered light of late summer sun
and the settling of mosquitoes
        under leaves
the cool of evening

in the board-room he whispers
under the rumble monotone purr
    a keyboard will get you half a gram
apparently you put it to a match :
collect the ashes
        smelt it at 1200°C
gives a knowing grin
leans in again
        the motherboard will get you a quarter

he's a prospector on the side
knows secret spots on the Fraser
        hidden entries
arteries of gold sifted through gravel
places where you can make a dollar
        knows spade
sweat and sore arms
the swirl-sounds on tin
knows the filtered light of dusk
    and the settling of mosquitoes
            under leaves
the cool of evening

in the board-room with the shuffle
and the scraping of chair legs
        he whispers
the man talking in front's a diesel purr
        motherboards get you a quarter gram
apparently you just put it to a match
collect the ashes
        smelt it at 1200°C
he gives a grin
his lips just wide enough to slip in a coin
leans in again
        keyboards get you half a gram

Part-Time Prospector

he's a prospector on the side
knows secret spots on all the rivers
          hidden entries
arteries of gold fingered in the gravel
places where you can make a buck or two
          knows spade
sweat and sore arms
the swirl-sounds on tin
knows the filtered light of dusk
the settling of mosquitoes
          under leaves
cool of evening

in the boardroom with the shuffle of papers
and the scraping of chair legs
          he whispers
the speaker up front's a diesel purr
          mother boards are worth a quarter gram
apparently you just put it to a match
collect all the ashes
fumes drifting off in the dark
          smelt it at 1200° C
he gives a grin
his lips just wide enough to slip in a coin
leans in again
          keyboards get you half

Part-Time Prospector
for Bob

he's a prospector on the side
knows secret spots on all the rivers
        hidden entries
arteries of gold fingered into the gravel
places where you can make a few dollars
        knows spade and sweat
the swirl-sounds on tin
knows the filtered sunlight of dusk
the settling of mosquitoes
        under leaves
the cool of evening

in the boardroom, under the shuffle of papers
and the scraping of chair legs
the room is filled with the speaker's diesel purr
like a generator that's too close to the camp
        he whispers: *motherboards get you a quarter gram*
you just put it to a match
collect the ashes
fumes drifting away in the dark
        smelt it at 1200 degrees
he gives a grin
his lips just wide enough to slip in a coin
leans in again
        keyboards are worth half a gram

Prospecteur à temps partiel
pour Bob

Traduit de l'anglais par Daniel Canty

il est prospecteur par penchant
connaît les recoins cachés des rivières
       les passages secrets
les artères d'or veinant le gravier
les endroits où empocher quelques dollars
       connaît la pelle et l'effort
le sifflement reptile de l'écuelle
connaît la lumière filtrée de la fin du jour
le sommeil des moustiques
       sous les feuillus
la fraîcheur du soir

dans le bureau chef, sous le froissement des papiers
et le craquement des pattes de chaise
la salle ronronne au diesel de ses paroles
un générateur trop proche du campement
       il murmure : *les cartes mères donnent un gramme*
on en approche une allumette
on recueille les cendres
les toxines s'envolent dans le noir
       en fusion à 1200 degrés
il sourit,
lèvres serrées où glisser un seul sou,
s'approche encore
       les claviers rapportent un demi gramme

Interview

1. What books, people, landscape, fuel your poetry?

Prince George lies somewhere between bush and inner city, between strip mall and urban pub, between mill and university, and all of it–the people, the weather, the consumption, the landscape–fuels my poetry. I've lived here the last fifteen years. To a lesser extent, my memories of Abbotsford, where I grew up, and other places in B.C., where I've travelled, have also turned into poems. I read as much contemporary poetry as I can get my hands on, and that provides a different sort of fuel.

2. How does a poem begin for you?

For me, poems start with an image, an idea, a turn of phrase, or more rarely, a structure. The first few drafts are forays into a forest that run deeper and deeper with each rewrite. Normally, all my drafts are written by hand except for the very last one. At some point the path finds itself, and becomes smoother with the travelling. These are the middle drafts. Near the end I make some kind of sign, a title, to say: This is where I've been.

3. What is the importance of poetry in society? In schools?

Society doesn't owe poets or poetry anything. Of course, I believe poetry is important–for seeing things in a new way, for opening our minds to new ideas, for interrogating our ways of being in the world, and for delving into the very nature of language, speech and thought; for students this can prove especially powerful as they come to terms with their existence in this world, with all of their ideas and emotions. However, poetry needs to find its own way in the world, and it will.

4. Will the internet and e-books ever replace the book for you as a poet?

Everyone seems worried about which new technologies will replace the old ones. The great thing about the internet is that it can deliver contemporary poetry the instant it's typed, provide poets a seemingly unlimited forum for publishing and poetics, and allow for new types of poetry. Let's have poems that appear on the page one word at a time. Let's have poems that cycle and morph in real-time. However, books still corner the market on a few things: their tactile nature, their aesthetic appeal, even their smell, as well as the way their text is read–the light reflected off the page, not emitted from a screen (which allows for longer reading times)–are too important to be left behind. For me, these qualities explain the longevity of this old technology. It may be that the publishers that succeed alongside the new technologies are the ones that make books delightful to hold, and that wouldn't be a bad thing.

Poetics

What a Poem Can Do

A poem can point–Here you go, here's a good place to start. A poem doesn't need to be "easy" or "hard." A poem can be itself. It can sing, chant or mumble. A poem can fit. Big in the waist for a belly full of ideas. Small as a dimple. A poem can surprise itself, either with wonder or fear. A poem can be comfortable with frayed edges and a hole in its elbow, knowing language is likewise torn. A poem can knock down. A poem can honour the weak. A poem can rage against injury. It can be complicit. A poem can contradict itself. It can pack a survival kit. Jot down a list. A poem can run away with itself. A poem invites others to make the same journey. Often they see what the poet hasn't. A poem can be quiet. It can falter. A poem can do many things, and what it can't do–that's for us to live.

Al Rempel

Al Rempel first started writing poetry in high school, in Abbotsford, where he was introduced to T.S. Eliot's "The Hollow Men" and William Blake's "Songs of Innocence & Experience." At the University of British Columbia, he continued to write while earning a Bachelor of Science with a major in physics, as well as during a Bachelor of Education. He met two friends in his dorm that were kind enough to mark up his poems in red ink. In 2000, Al went to the Victoria School of Writing, where Sue Wheeler encouraged him to send his work to various journals. He was published in *Grain* and then in *The Malahat Review*, as well as in a few anthologies–most recently in *Rocksalt*. He's also tried his hand at two chapbooks. Al has been very thankful for the writing groups he's been a part of because his fellow poets continue to write ink all over his poems. The latest group has been called "candlefish, etc, etc," and all of its members have recently been published.

ACKNOWLEDGEMENTS

'A Few Lines for Prince George' was first published in *The Malahat Review*. 'Part-Time Prospector' and 'Saskatchewan Glacier' were previously anthologized in *The Forest Diversification Project*, UNBC Press.

Thank-you to Jayson Hencheroff of Focal Point Studios for the photograph and Daniel Canty for the French translation of 'Part-Time Prospector'.

ONJANA YAWNGHWE

To my family

moving earth

1.

I crack earth open with a shovel,
a rain-sunk mound crusted over,
slow hard-baking in ovened summer;
the taste of rain dangles in the wind,
sky turns over, distends its grey belly
wide touching the ragged tips of mountains.

The sharp outpour of metal slices
as I bend down and upturn my scoopful:
as if the soil is frosting up eggs,
the ground bubbles with rocks,
a few fist-heavy, numerous smaller
all sprout up greeting air.
I stop for a moment, realizing how hard
it will be to make my mother a garden.

2.

She spends forever leaving home
she needs this narrow piece of earth,
to know one armful of land is for her.

She witnesses Burma change from white-gloved
British hands meticulously picking rubies from the land,
to clouded Japanese faces drooping with hunger and war
to the confused, brutal fists of her countrymen,
all rebel-hungry and wanting
and that land is squeezed starving by men
who cling to guns with one hand and cover
their eyes with the other so they won't see what
their army boots and trigger fingers are doing.
The country is shut off.
Blood everywhere.

Her hands too are soaked in blood
she, my father, and the exhausted people
the government thought they'd beaten
down rust-coloured mud fight back,
but nothing changes, smallness raised
against enormity is ground down.
She escapes to Thailand and mimes a life;
she comes to Canada and does the same.

3.

Kneeling on loosened earth,
my hands enter coolness,
I shift one handful of dirt
to another, sifting stones.
Rocks pant as they rub each other
the damp smell of shaded trees
wind breathing round branches
the old years of being here.

It's been a long time
since I've touched earth.

4.

Six years old, I dig just for digging,
not with sharp metal but with sticks
and with fingernails, hard and tanned,
I discover the colours of the land:

Chiang Mai in my backyard,
the ground is dust and a yellow that doesn't shine
and hands are powdered in an instant
and yellow turns molten gold in hot palms.

Deeper, earth becomes wetter and cooler,
clay redder and denser than chili paste
my skin is finger-painted fire
I taste it to see if it would burn
but my mouth grows sudden cool and
I'm in a cave, smelling wet, rain, rock.
I rub my lips with red and become nature-beautiful
for that instant ready to be woman-new even though
I'm still a girl, I'll hold to my chest bleeding rubies,
dark histories my mother wore bursting from lips and fingertips.

Next layer is like death
dark brown, almost black
cold of cut bones.
I dig and dig and it never ends
my stick is frozen
I am afraid to touch it.
I stare at the small hole
yellow, red, then black.

5.

Blackness pushes under my fingernails
dampness floods beneath my skin
I push open more soil, heavy persuasion:
more stones like baby potatoes burst up,
coated with coarse and moist darkness
The smell of slowness covers everything,
penetrates my palms and fingers into rivers.

All things natural must smell like this,
of soil, bark, rotten fruit, rain and even clouds,
of night with its heart-rounding scent of closeness,
long faded stars which loiter still clinging to their bodies,
the vague stinging salt of the sea patting cheeks red
exuding from coupled-skins in close-clasping darkness.
This odour of permanence, of always being.

6.

Wispy-thin roots delicately tangle in earth,
sprouts like winding roads gleam pure white,
nuggets of red cedar nestle, some spliced lined and rotting,
some whittled down in dirt-muscle to a whirling top,
some spare and dry as ocean driftwood bleached pale,
some mimicking a scrap of human spine.
Armored insects no bigger than a point on a page
swiftly scramble between hollows of soil, up
spider-legged moss, hairy wet and molded yellow
while one thin red worm coils itself into a knot
while another stretches out bloated and heavy,
mottled purple squirms up S-shapes as I shovel
all this up and lay it over new, level ground.

7.

I am expecting waist-deep snow
so cold it burns but this is vancouver
and it happens to be august and the streets are grey
not white and hard with sun and the concrete rasps.
We live in a three-part beige apartment complex
in mount pleasant and I don't talk to anybody
because I'm afraid and I can't speak english or
smile in english but I learn and little girls ask me
why my lips are so huge my nose so flat why
so beady eyes and all the while I'm expecting snow.
Mom works all day first at mcdonald's then as a maid
she is no longer a school teacher instead she
cleans people's toilets and mops floors
wet rags in her hands, knees touching tile.

We only touch processed grey and pass by grass
growing in rectangles along sidewalks and they rise
in brittle yellow points and threaten holes in our feet;
sometimes we see hand-stretching roses or dahlias
which are always mysteriously bright pink.
I like dandelions which grow free and spontaneous
in places people don't want them to, and they beam
like shaken suns, globe-change quickly and I help them
blow away by vigorously kicking them airborne and
watch seeds like parachuting snowflakes
search for a bit of land to make a home on,
to ground down roots that will stick no matter
how many people try to pull them out.

8.

Earth remembers hands that touch it,
that stroke its curves and curl against its body,
that caress its fine hair of roots and petal-lips,
that gently part open its ankles, knees and thighs,
cleaving soft fluffy soil with two palms pressed
and bury a snowflake which quickly disappears
down past rocks, worms, and bone-shaped wood.

It recalls the abrupt depressions of flesh,
of nameless bodies collapsing in reddened mud
of them who vanish suddenly from homes
who spend their last few seconds cradled by this soil.
Of them who remain behind to remember.

9.

Her voice low and slow, breathing in music,
she tells me of Shan State, how it wore chill by day,
not the sun-flamed robes of the sweltering south,
how raw mist would ride over the valley and lag,
leave skin glistening like it'd been dipped in stars.
Of certain leaves which taste bitter against your teeth
but soon a sweetness lingers softly round the tongue,
so you only recall the mouth-filling sugar of longing.

How the cold-tinged air hangs slow and ripe with jasmine,
white blossoms as large as her father's hands,
so many she can hardly see green within;
mornings her fingers gently pick the flowers,
pull them until they release themselves
into her clay bowl, so large and earth-heavy
she has to stretch wide her small embrace.
Holding smells to her skin with thin arms.

10.

Between her words, the roll and tumble of them,
the way they come out singing the same song,
her memories drop like rice before my feet
· Shan tea mountain breath in my ear
from her hair the odor of rust, of earth
the scent of blood she'd held in her hands
the tongue hidden beneath the soil
the dream the darkness in her eyes
an amazon of leaves gleaming blackness,
her body the moist naked ground.
Roots gather at the touch of her words.

11.

I dream mango trees are growing in my backyard
drooping heavy with fruit stubbornly sour-hard
tall banana trees sprout up crunchy and green,
their arms glossing light and flapping like flags;
at earth-level, round mushrooms like black pebbles
murmur beneath tree-shade, nesting in silky soil;
I eat them again, drop them raw into my mouth,
each mushroom-marble pops between my teeth
and I'm eating firecrackers and earth, in my cheeks
stones drop into a well of water in moonlight,
echo off my teeth and plunge down my throat.
I dream of so many things.

12.

grip stones

touch water

heavy and solid enter my hot fist
the stones drag cool my blood

air weaves through fingers
swirls in palms even as
hand grips stones tight

I hold a forest iced by night,
the breath of northern seas
stroking beyond the horizon,
steady moon-shadows gliding
across light-brindled Inle Lake.

I wait for my fist to warm the stones.
They stay cool long after
my patience
runs out.

13.

Skies stoop low, the air sweats,
oceans roll in clouds as grey trembles;
rain falls as I step under a nearby tree.
The pile of stones shiver as a push of wind
runs through the branches, shakes from its leaves
fluttering raindrops that flicker like jewels.
Pebbles bathe and glaze with wet colour,
soil breathes water and steams,
the pungent sharpness of bruised roots rises,
grass deepens green and high above me,
young cherries shine red and taut.

I hear water drumming the leaves,
rattling stones, gently sucked down
earth by low, thirsty spider-web roots.

I put aside the shovel
and inhale slowness.

I smell mint and jasmine that will grow here,
rust musk of sandalwood dwelling with cedar;
the scent rubs on my fingers,
echoes everywhere.

The dirt, pebbles, trees tell me to take my time,
as rain shivers and drops as if suspended in air,
as roots follow the low-curved cadence of waiting
and the soaked air brims clouds to a falling fullness;
as long as I touch earth I'm planting home
seeding memories, even those that are not my own.

lost again

lost again

after visiting the internet café in Khampaeng Phet
I try to return to the guest house, but spend
hours wandering empty streets

stray dogs and fenced houses
everywhere dogs bark
a brown poodle and a terrier chase me
nip at my pant legs

finally I spot a thin old man driving
his scooter cart and hitch a ride
balancing among bags of rice

*

the Buddha Chinnarat sits as if soaked in morning
gold that shines and softens like a feathered sun
spires arise from his body, rising he sits
serenely smiling in the middle of flames

later I learn how to catch fish
with a small trap of thorns

walking by the dark green Nan river I see
a hundred middle-aged men and women
in red and blue and yellow sweatsuits
moving arms legs in aerobic unison
to the wild blasting electronic beat of
Kylie's "I just can't get you outta my head"

*

a room with a bed
and a ceiling fan

empty bottles of water
the dull linoleum floor

the day's discards
pages of *The Bangkok Post*
scattered on the bedspread

surprising
that I long so
for home here

my Canada

Ghost

DRAFTS, FINISHED POEM AND TRANSLATION INTO THAI

What the night says *[handwritten: good title? why this title?]*

[handwritten: a bit awkward / what do you mean?]

[handwritten left margin: too colloquial?]

    remember that little short-legged girl
      with big bangs and bowl haircut *[handwritten: physical picture of the girl? why?]*
  nope didn't talk much but when
she let loose boy you could hear her *[handwritten: girl-boy]*

remember how the heat feels around your body *[handwritten: no - something else]* *[handwritten: you need to go back & remember]*
    how it pushes you a little   and slows you
        your movement   to   the pace of clouds
the sky how it first licks your skin and
          surrounds
           like a long arm moving in water *[handwritten: yes - like it.]*

remember your first tongue the first letters
  your pencil formed in your school notebook
the words your hands were trained to write *[handwritten: no - something else]*
    the sounds that first came from your throat
[handwritten: birthed from] round letters the curved vowels that cupped
[handwritten: alphabet] your chin and held you so close to its belly *[handwritten: why belly.]*

               the first mother *[handwritten: who is speaking?]*
               you ran away from

[handwritten: movement rethink / why does it look like that / on the page?]

Caps — rethink title again

Ghost

needs space + breath

is she asking? what are you trying to say?

do you remember that bucking girl with the bangs, and bowl in her hands, ~~didn't talk much but~~ *redundant* always listening to the sound of bees kicking nectar from flowers and cats licking the salt from rocks

repeat   too domestic another animal?

do you remember how the heat pushes your head down, and slows your movement to the pace of clouds, (long arm moving in water) how warmth surrounds you like a cat sleeping, chilies circling the belly   *air + water · too far?*

do you remember (first tongue,) the first letters your pencil traced in your notebook, sounds birthed in the throat, round alphabet and curved vowels that cupped your chin and held you so close

I was the first mother you ran away from.

like "English Lesson"

too many words? dense.

(ghost) title ?

space

~~do you remember~~ that bucking girl with the bangs ~~and bowl in her hands,~~ always listening to the sound of bees kicking nectar from flowers and bare snakes licking the salt off rocks

~~do you remember how the~~ heat pushes your head down, and slows your movement to the pace of clouds, how warmth surrounds you like a cat sleeping chilies circling the belly

~~do you remember the~~ first letters your pencil traced in your notebook sounds birthed in the throat, round alphabet and curved vowels that cupped your chin and held you so close

I was the first mother
you ran away from.

it is time to strip it all away

what else — more, 1 got elementary
she is close to earth?
animals, a fellow
creature himself
— language as nature

in the mirror you wanted a
different face looking back at you

silent because angry

we never knew
about
what you left behind
you troubled + squeezed
stones into your fins

ghost

that bucking girl

              with the bangs

        sharp sticks in her hand

       she listens to the sound of bees

        kicking nectar from flowers

            bare snakes licking the salt off rocks

(In the mirror you wanted)

     how the heat

          pushes your head down

    slows your movement   to the pace of clouds

how warmth surrounds you like a sleeping cat

             chilies circling its belly

(a different face looking back at you.)

    the first letters   traced in the dirt

            sounds birthed in the throat

   round alphabet   curved vowels

       that cupped your chin and held you so close

I was the first mother
you ran away from.

วิญญาณ

(Translated by Sangkhue Preraputtiwong)

เด็กหญิงน่ารำคาญ
ไว้ผมหน้าม้า

กิ่งไม้แหลมในมือของเธอ

ฟังเสียงของฝูงผึ้ง

แตะถึบน้ำหวานจากดอกไม้

งูรอกคราบเลียเกลือจากก้อนหิน

(ในกระจกที่เธอต้องการ)

เมื่อความร้อน
ผลักดันศีรษะเธอลง

การเคลื่อนไหวช้าลง   เท่าเทียมก้อนเมฆ

เมื่อความอบอุ่นครอบคลุมตัวเธอเหมือนแมวนอนหลับ
ความเยือกเย็นเข้ารอบท้องน้อยข
องมัน

(หลายคนมองกลับมาที่เธอ)

อักษรตัวแรก   ทิ้งร้องรอนบนผืนดิน

เสียงเล็ดรอดออกจากลำคอ

ตัวอักษรกลม   ตัวสระโค้งรอบ

นั่นกลุ่มคางของเธอและยึดเธอไว้แนบชิด

ฉันคือแม่คนแรก
ที่เธอหนีจากไป

Interview

1. When did you begin to write poetry and what inspired you to continue?

I began to seriously write poetry when I was in university, though a few years ago I came across a hand-printed little book of about ten poems that I'd apparently made when I was eight or nine years old. I had no memory of it—it was a bit of an odd Borges moment, like I was meeting an entirely different version of myself. Anyway, throughout my life I'd kept these detailed journals, so I was used to writing, but the writing of poetry came suddenly, as in a flood. I remember lying in bed and out of nowhere surged this incredible need to write a poem, so I sat in front of my typewriter and just typed for hours. Of course, these first works weren't very good, but it became the way for me.

I'm inspired by other poems and poets. When I read a remarkable poem I'm just in awe at the possibilities of words, and what they can do emotionally and intellectually. It makes me want to be able to create something that beautiful. Plus, I don't think I can stop writing poetry. I've had long dry spells, and when I'm not writing I'm the most miserable person on the planet! Sometimes I paint, make little books, or sew to assuage that creative need, but I feel the most complete when I'm writing poetry.

2. What is the importance of poetry in society? In schools?

I feel that poetry is a kind of refuge from a world that's getting faster and more impatient. Poems carve out a space for themselves; they provide a return to silence. Each poem is an invitation to enter into its world, and really reading a poem takes a measure of effort, concentration and calm—it requires a kind of surrender. To me, reading a poem is a kind of meditation: you become aware of the words and the sounds they are creating in your mind, the blank spaces of the in-between spaces. You come into yourself as you enter the entirely different context of the poem, and in that moment, you feel most alive and present.

Poetry in schools is important—I think children should be read poems from the very beginning, because it seems that children have this natural attraction for some of the elements of poetry—rhyme, rhythm, assonance, alliteration are all present in Dr. Seuss or nursery rhymes. I'm not sure how poetry became so unused after such a promising beginning. Students should have more exposure to all kinds of poetry—I remember being taught Frost and Dickinson and having no idea that people still wrote poetry, that it was still alive! Once students are more exposed to poetry, they will find a way into the poem, and poetry will become such a resource to return to later on.

3. Who are your favourite poets?

Here's a very abbreviated list:
Galway Kinnell, *The Book of Nightmares*; Dionne Brand, *Land to Light On*; Anne
Carson; Fred Wah; Sylvia Plath; Christina Rossetti, *Sing-Song*; John Thompson, *Stilt
Jack*; Phyllis Webb, *Water and Light*; Betsy Warland; Jeanette Armstrong, *Breath
Tracks*; Roy Kiyooka; Jan Kaplinski, *Through the Forest*; Marilyn Dumont; Tim
Lilburn, *To the River.*

4. What do you envision for the future of poetry?

Well, I hope that poetry has a very bright future. I realize most people don't read
poetry and view poetry as some rarefied, incomprehensible thing, but I hope more
people give it a chance. I wish more and more people would buy poetry books,
borrow them from the library, revive the industry. I know there are poems out there
that will speak to each person in a most profound way, but the trick is finding that
poem or poet. It's in some ways like finding someone and falling in love, except much
easier!

I also like where poetry is heading—there are so many small publishers and
micropresses out there and really, it's become like blogging—anyone can create his
or her own chapbook or journal. It's very democratic at that level. There are some
incredible works of art that result from these home-made efforts.

I think that the wealth and varieties of poetry are astounding—though visual and
sound poetry has a lengthy history, what's out there is amazing, really blurring the
edges between music, art, poetry.

Poetics

Poetry is intersection—all the minute occurrences, permutations of chance, that lead to this specific and particular junction of this present moment. And each person is the history of those who came before—parents, grandparents, ancestors from the beginning of human time; chemically, we carry their stories in bones and blood. We are made of so many endless generations. We are also at the nexus of multiple landscapes: places where we were born, raised, moved to and from, visited, and each place has been imprinted upon us, and imprinted onto those who came before us. The air, the water, the light upon the skin—all have composed us. This is where words come from, the distillation of these pluralities. When we speak a poem, the words vibrate in our flesh, and reverberate in the multiple histories that compose us. When I write about an experience, the words aren't actually about me—they are parts of a larger story, of the many lives and many other lands, from Shan State, Burma, to Thailand, Canada, Europe and innumerable other landscapes. I've always been very curious about how one can enter a poem so completely; poetry has the unique power of simultaneously expressing the unique person while allowing the reader to enter into someone else's landscape and history. It encourages the fluid movement between identities, how one can look at words on a page and simply let go. You read the poem, the poem reads you.

Onjana Yawnghwe

Although her family is originally from Shan State in Burma, Onjana Yawnghwe was born in Chiang Mai, Thailand, and came to Canada at the age of seven. She grew up in Vancouver and Coquitlam, and received both a Bachelor's and Master's degree in English from *UBC*. She has been published in various literary journals and anthologies, and also dabbles occasionally in book design. She is also the co-editor of *Xerography*, a little literary journal and the co-founder of *fish magic press*, a micropress that specializes in unique, hand-made chapbooks. She currently lives in Burnaby with fellow writer and husband, Shane, and nonwriter Pique the Cat. When not writing, Onjana paints, sews, makes block and screen prints, and is always learning to play the ukulele and the game of Go.

ACKNOWLEDGEMENTS

An earlier version of poems #2,4,5 of 'moving earth' were published in *Grain*, 29.2, 2001. 'lost again' is part of a long poem called "Thai Suites" which was published by Ricepaper, issue 14.1.

Thank-you to Sangkhue Preraputtiwong for her translation of 'ghost'.

Thanks

To Robert Hilles and Lorraine Gane for editing and copyediting assistance.
To the photographers: Frank Lee, Jayson Hencheroff, Shane Plante and David Kong.
To Joe Rosenblatt for his new drawings and to Ian Thomas for his painting on the cover.
To Mark Hand for his design and to Shari MacDonald for photographing Ian's painting.
To the translators Daniel Canty, Sangkhue Preraputtiwong, Peter Morin and Daniela Elza, and Elena E. Johnson for her reading of French. And to Gerhard Aichelberger, our Freisens representative.

Daniel Canty is a writer, director and translator living in Montreal. His translation of Stephanie Bolster's Alice poems, *Pierre Blanche* (Le Noroît, 2007) won a rare honourable mention from the John Glasscoe prize jury. He is currently working on a French translation of Charles Simic's *Dime-Store Alchemy, The Art of Joseph Cornell*.

Sangkhue Preraputtiwong was raised in Chiang Mai, Thailand and graduated with a Nursing degree from the University of Chiang Mai. Now living in Canada Sangkhue will graduate as a Registered Nurse in July, 2009.

Joe Rosenblatt makes no distinction between his visual art and his poetry and has held on to this mindset since the early seventies. He has exhibited in many galleries and has won the Governor General's Award for Poetry as well as B.C.'s Dorothy Livesay Poetry Prize. His most recent book is *Dog* (Mansfield Press, 2008), collaborative sonnets with Catherine Owen. He lives in Qualicum Beach with his wife Faye and his three cats. Titles for his drawings: *Lady and Butterflies*-p.vi, *Blackbirds*-p.1, *Old Tree*-p.28, *Bird Spirits*-p.29, *Minimalist Bird*-p.58, *Qualicum Woods*-p.59, *Hamilton Marsh*-p.75, *Qualicum Woods, Noon*-p.85.'

Ian Thomas has a long history as both teacher and artist. His childhood was spent in Brighton, England, and he later graduated from Birmingham College of Art. He taught at UBC in the Faculty of Education and in the Visual Arts Department at Camosun College. He lives and has his studio on Salt Spring Island.

More acknowledgements under Poets' bios.